MY FIRST BRITANNICA

The Earth
and Earth Sciences

1

ENCYCLOPÆDIA
Britannica®

CHICAGO   LONDON   NEW DELHI   PARIS   SEOUL   SYDNEY   TAIPEI   TOKYO

© 2004 by Encyclopædia Britannica, Inc.

International Standard Book Number: 1-59339-048-3 (set)
International Standard Book Number: 1-59339-049-1 (volume 1)

My First Britannica:
Volume 1: The Earth and Earth Sciences 2004

Britannica.com may be accessed on the Internet at http://www.britannica.com.

The Earth and Earth Sciences

TABLE OF CONTENTS

Lightning storm, Tucson, Arizona
© Tom Ives/Corbis

The Earth and Earth Sciences

INTRODUCTION

What's another name for giant floating ice cubes?

How did the dinosaurs disappear? Is a 'finger of land' smaller than your hand?

What's an oasis?

In Volume 1, *The Earth and Earth Sciences,* you'll discover answers to these questions and many more. Through pictures, articles, and fun facts, you'll learn about weather, study oceans and landscapes, and go back in time to the days of the dinosaurs.

To help you on your journey, we've provided the following signposts in *The Earth and Earth Sciences*:

■ **Subject Tabs**—The coloured box in the upper corner of each right-hand page will quickly tell you the article subject.

■ **Search Lights**—Try these mini-quizzes before and after you read the article and see how much - *and how quickly* - you can learn. You can even make this a game with a reading partner. (Answers are upside down at the bottom of one of the pages.)

■ **Did You Know?**—Check out these fun facts about the article subject. With these surprising 'factoids', you can entertain your friends, impress your teachers, and amaze your parents.

■ **Picture Captions**—Read the captions that go with the photos. They provide useful information about the article subject.

■ **Vocabulary**—New or difficult words are in **bold type**. You'll find them explained in the Glossary at the back of this volume. And there's a complete listing of all Glossary terms in the set in the *Reference Guide and Index*, Volume 13.

■ **Learn More!**—Follow these pointers to related articles throughout the set.

And don't forget: If you're not sure where to start, where you saw something before, or where to go next, the *Reference Guide and Index* (Volume 13) will point the way.

Have a great trip!

MY FIRST BRITANNICA

Learning About the Earth

Geography is the science of the Earth's surface. It helps us learn about what makes the different shapes and colours of the Earth - the ground, rocks, and water, what does and does not grow.

If you look at the Earth as a geographer does, then you might see it as a colourful map. Much more than half of it is blue with oceans, lakes, rivers, and streams. In some places it is tan-coloured with the sands of dry deserts. In other places it is green with forests. There are purple-grey mountains and white snow-capped peaks. And there are the soft yellow of grain fields and the light green of leafy crops.

Part of learning about the Earth is learning where people can and can't live. The different colours of your Earth map can help you discover this.

You won't find many people in the tan, white, or larger blue parts - deserts, the snowfields, and oceans. Not many people live in the deserts, because deserts are hot and dry. Very few plants can grow there. In the high mountains and at the North and South poles, it is very cold. Most plants don't like the cold, and most people don't either.

You will find people in and near the green and yellow parts and the smaller blue parts - the farmlands, forests, rivers, and lakes. To those regions you can add brown dots and clusters of dots, for towns and cities.

There's a lot to learn about the Earth, just as there's a lot to learn about a friend. Geography helps you become the Earth's friend.

LEARN MORE! READ THESE ARTICLES...
CONTINENTS (VOLUME 1) • FERDINAND MAGELLAN (VOLUME 4)
OCEANS (VOLUME 1)

The coast of Nova Scotia, in Canada, shows some of Earth's many shapes and colours. Geography looks closely at what makes these different shapes and colours.
© Raymond Gehman/Corbis

DID YOU KNOW?
The 'big blue marble' is one nickname for the planet Earth. This is because, from space, our world looks like a big round marble - all blue with swirling white streaks of clouds.

SEARCH LIGHT

Areas where
not many people
live are also the
areas where few
plants grow. Why do
you think that is?
(Hint: What do you do
with lettuce, beans,
and apples?)

Answer: If few plants grow in an area, then few animals will live
there. This is because animals need either plants or other animals
to eat. And without plants or animals, there's nothing for people
to eat.

The Largest Pieces of Land

NORTH AMERICA

The continents are the largest bodies of land on the Earth. Look at a globe. Whatever is blue is water. Most of the rest is land: the continents.

There are seven continents. From biggest to smallest, they are Asia, Africa, North America, South America, Antarctica, Europe, and Australia.

Some continents, such as Australia and Antarctica, are completely surrounded by water. And some continents are joined together, as Asia and Europe are.

Continents are physical bodies, defined by their shape, size, and location. They have mountains, rivers, deserts, forests, and other physical features. But people have divided them into **political** groupings, called 'countries' or 'nations'.

Large continents, such as Asia, may include both very large countries, such as China, and very small countries, such as Nepal. Australia, the smallest continent, is also a country - one of the world's largest.

North America contains three countries: Canada, the United States, and Mexico - and a few small countries in a region known as Central America. Europe, on the other hand, is the world's second-smallest continent but has about 50 countries.

Africa, the second-largest continent, is believed to be where the very first humans appeared. The continent of Antarctica is all by itself down at the South Pole. It is rocky and is covered by thick ice that never melts. Only a few plants and animals can be found along its seacoasts.

Earth scientists believe that the continents began forming billions of years ago. Lighter parts of Earth's **molten** core separated from heavier parts and rose to the top. As they cooled off and became solid, the land that eventually became the continents formed.

Most scientists agree that the individual continents were at first joined together and then drifted apart. One theory suggests that there were once two 'supercontinents': Gondwanaland in the south and Laurasia in the north.

LEARN MORE! READ THESE ARTICLES...
AFRICA (VOLUME 8) • AUSTRALIA (VOLUME 7) • EUROPE (VOLUME 6)

SEARCH LIGHT

Name the seven continents.

SOUTH AMERICA

EUROPE

ASIA

AFRICA

AUSTRALIA

ANTARCTICA

DID YOU KNOW?
Here's a silly rhyme to help you remember the continents:
Africa is hot,
Antarctica is cold.
Asia is crowded,
Europe is old.
There's an America down South,
and one up North too,
And Australia has the kangaroo.

Answer: Africa, Antarctica, Asia, Australia, North America, South America, and Europe.

A Continent of Extremes

Antarctica is the coldest, windiest, and highest **continent** in the world. It lies at the bottom of the world, surrounding the South Pole. The name Antarctica means 'opposite to the Arctic', referring to the Arctic Circle on the other side of the world.

The coldest temperature recorded in Antarctica is also the world's lowest, at −89.2°C. A sheet of ice covers the entire continent. At its thickest point, the ice is almost 5 kilometres deep - and that's on *top* of the ground. The continent contains most of the world's ice and much of the world's freshwater. Toward the edges of the continent, the ice becomes glaciers, creeping rivers of ice.

Strange and wonderful Antarctica has only one day in the entire year. The Sun generally rises on 21 September and sets on 22 March. This one long day is the summer. From 22 March until 21 September, the South Pole is dark and Antarctica has its night, or winter.

People do not live permanently in Antarctica. Only scientists and some adventurous tourists visit. There are, however, 45 species of birds in

DID YOU KNOW?
Antarctica is a desert - a 'frigid desert'. It's extremely cold, unlike the more common hot sandy deserts. But like them, it gets so little moisture during the year that very little life can survive.

Antarctica, including the emperor penguin and the Adélie penguin, that live near the seacoast. Also, four species of seals breed only in Antarctica.

Whales live in the water around the **frigid** continent. The killer whale, the sperm whale, the rare bottle-nosed whale, the pygmy whale, and seven species of baleen whales can all be found off the coast.

Oddly, there are active volcanoes in Antarctica. That means you can find not just the world's coldest temperatures here but, deep down, some of the hottest too.

LEARN MORE! READ THESE ARTICLES...
GLACIERS (VOLUME 1) • PENGUINS (VOLUME 11)
WHALES (VOLUME 12)

These emperor penguins are some of Antarctica's very few inhabitants. So in a way, they might indeed be considered the 'rulers' of this harsh and beautiful frozen desert continent.
© Galen Rowell/Corbis

SEARCH LIGHT

Match the numbers with the correct labels. You may have to do some working out and clever thinking!

45	coldest temperature
−89.2	bird species
182.5	thickness of ice
5	length of one day

Answer: −89.2 (°C) — coldest temperature
45 — bird species
5 (kilometres) — thickness of ice
182.5 (days) — length of one day

Dry Spots in a Watery World

SEARCH LIGHT

Find and correct the error in the following sentence: Coral islands are made of tiny ocean rocks that have piled on top of each other for thousands of years.

Islands are areas of land surrounded on all sides by water. Islands come in all shapes and sizes. The very smallest are too small to hold even a house. The largest islands contain whole countries.

If you live in the United Kingdom, Iceland, Australia, or Japan, you live on an island. But these islands are so large that you might walk all day and never see water.

How do islands develop in the first place?

Some islands begin as fiery volcanoes in the ocean. Hot lava pours out of the volcano, making the island bigger and bigger. Slowly, as the lava cools, it becomes solid land, and when it rises above the water, it becomes an island. These are the volcanic islands.

Small island in the South Pacific Ocean.
© Craig Tuttle/Corbis

Other islands are actually parts of the world's **continents**. Some of the land towards the edge of the continent may have been worn away over many, many years by wind or rain, or perhaps some of it sank. Then water from the ocean came in to fill the low places and made a new island.

A row of islands may once have been the tops of mountains in a mountain range. The Aleutian Islands off the coast of North America were probably once a part of a mountain range that connected Alaska with Asia.

Perhaps most surprising are the islands that are built up from the bottom of the ocean from the skeletons of tiny, tiny sea animals called 'coral'. As some corals die, others live on top of them. After thousands of years, a coral island rises to the ocean surface. And these islands go on living!

LEARN MORE! READ THESE ARTICLES...
CORAL (VOLUME 11) • SEYCHELLES (VOLUME 8) • VOLCANOES (VOLUME 1)

This photo from the air shows one of the islands of the Maldives, a country made up of about 1,300 islands in the Indian Ocean.
© Lawson Wood/Corbis

DID YOU KNOW?
If you try to count the number of islands in the world by looking at a globe, you'll probably come up with 300 or so. But that's only the major islands. Altogether the total is closer to 130,000.

Answer: Coral islands are made of tiny ocean creatures [or creatures' skeletons] that have piled on top of each other for thousands of years.

Mountains of Smoke and Fire

Deep under the Earth's surface, it's so hot that even rock melts. Sometimes this molten rock, called 'magma', is pushed up to the surface. At this point it is referred to as 'lava'. And the opening or vent that lets the lava out is a volcano.

A volcano may explode violently, throwing out rocks for miles around. Or it may push lava out so that it flows away, cools, and hardens. Some volcanoes release clouds of poisonous gas or huge clouds of ash. Volcanoes can even do all these things underwater.

Most volcanoes have been around for a very long time. Many haven't erupted for years and have cooled off. Volcanoes that are not going to erupt again are called 'dead volcanoes'.

Some volcanoes still give off smoke. These 'sleeping volcanoes' may 'wake up' one day and erupt again. Mount Vesuvius in Italy slept for a thousand years. But one day in AD 79 it suddenly woke up. Its eruption hurled out hot ash and rocky fragments that buried the city of Pompeii. A hot mudflow buried nearby Herculaneum. Because the remains are so well preserved, the area has been named a World Heritage site.

But not all volcanoes are destructive. When a volcano throws out vast amounts of lava and **debris**, it piles up into a mountain. The Hawaiian Islands and the island of Iceland were created in this way.

Other volcanoes help provide heat and energy. Many Icelandic homes get their hot water from springs heated by volcanic steam. This steam can also be used to produce electricity. Plants grow very well in the rich soil left by volcanoes. And valuable gems, such as diamonds, can sometimes be found in the rocks that are thrown out by volcanoes.

SEARCH LIGHT

Which of the following is *not* produced by volcanoes?

a) lava   d) ash
b) oil   e) steam
c) gas

LEARN MORE! READ THESE ARTICLES...
MOUNTAINS (VOLUME 1) • NICARAGUA (VOLUME 9) • REYKJAVIK (VOLUME 6)

Building Earth's Giant Landscapes

What makes mountains? Several different processes contribute to mountain building. And most mountains are formed by a combination of these - usually over millions of years.

Deep inside, the Earth is so incredibly hot that everything is melted, or molten. This molten material, or lava, escapes to the Earth's surface when volcanoes erupt. The lava cools and becomes hard and solid. This happens again and again, collecting until there is a volcanic mountain.

Mount Fuji in Japan and Mount St. Helens in Washington state, U.S., are volcanic mountains. There are also many undersea volcanic mountains - much taller than anything on land!

In some cases, strong earthquakes caused the surface rock for miles and miles to break. Part of the surface was then lower and part of it was higher. More earthquakes moved the lower parts down and the upper parts up. Eventually, the high parts became tall enough to make mountains.

Still other mountains were pushed up from the bottom of an ocean when two enormous portions of the Earth crashed together - *very slowly*, over millions and millions of years. Some of the largest mountain chains formed this way. The Andes of South America is an example.

Another mountain-building process is called 'folding'. If you push a rug up against a wall, it folds and rumples. That's basically the way the Appalachian Mountains in eastern North America were formed.

At first, most mountains were steep and sharp. But even hard rocks can be worn away. Slowly, with the wind and the rain rubbing at them, steep sharp mountains grew smoother, shorter, and rounder.

> **Mountains are made when**
> a) volcanoes erupt.
> b) earthquakes happen.
> c) the Earth pushes together.
> d) all of the above.

LEARN MORE! READ THESE ARTICLES…
ANDES (VOLUME 9) • TENZING NORGAY (VOLUME 4)
VOLCANOES (VOLUME 1)

DID YOU KNOW?
To be considered a mountain, the land must rise at least 610 metres above its surroundings. Mount Everest, the world's highest mountain, rises 8,850 metres above sea level.

The Nitty-Gritty

You can find sand at the edge of lakes, the bottoms of rivers, and the seaside. You can find it in mountain valleys, deserts, and of course a sandpit. Where does all this sand come from?

Sand is created when rocks break into tiny, tiny pieces. For example, wind, ice, and rain knock against high mountain cliffs. Slowly, over millions of years, these forces break off pieces of rock. The pieces bounce down the mountainside and break off other pieces of rock - while they're also breaking into smaller and smaller pieces themselves. This isn't sand yet, but it's getting there.

Rivers and glaciers are also good at making sand. A river's water rushes along, carrying rocks with it and breaking them into little pieces. The ice of a glacier grinds away at the rocks it slowly moves across.

Another great sand maker is the ocean. Every day, all over the world, tides rise and fall, pushing against rocks over and over. Waves tear at the rocks along the shore, wearing them down.

Thanks to the weather, water, and ice, some of these broken rocks finally get so small that they become what we call 'sand'.

Now that you have all this sand, what can you do with it? Sand is used for paving roads. Bricks made with sand are harder and stronger than other bricks. Sand is also used to filter (or clean) water. When it's sprayed with great force against stone or brick, it can grind away thick layers of dirt or paint through a process called 'sandblasting'.

And, of course, sand is great for building sandcastles!

LEARN MORE! READ THESE ARTICLES…
ALGERIA (VOLUME 8) • DESERTS (VOLUME 1) • OCEANS (VOLUME 1)

SEARCH LIGHT

True or false? Sand can be used to clean buildings.

Mounds or ridges of sand like these are called 'sand dunes'. They're caused by the combined action of wind and gravity.
© Dave G. Houser/Corbis

DID YOU KNOW?
Once a year the Harrison Hot Springs resort in British Columbia, Canada, holds the world sand sculpting championship. The rules say sculptures can be made only of water and sand, and they must be finished in under 100 work hours.

Answer: TRUE. Sandblasting is a powerful process for cleaning stone or brick.

Lands of Little Water

Deserts are places that get very little rain each year - so little rain that most trees and plants cannot grow there. Some deserts will go for years without rain. They are difficult places to live in, and the few plants,

Golden desert snapdragons, or yellow Mojave flowers, in Death Valley, California, U.S.
© Darrell Gulin/Corbis

animals, and people who live there have to be tough to survive. Every continent except Europe has a desert. Even Antarctica has one, a **frigid** desert.

Most deserts, however, are arid or dry deserts with mile after mile of sand, baked earth, and barren rock. In the daytime, these places look like lost worlds - hot, dry, and silent. Usually, the only plants growing there are low thorny ones. These plants store most of the water they are able to collect. It may be a long time before their next drink.

At night it can be quite cold in the desert. That's when creatures that have been hiding from the Sun's burning rays come out of their homes. Many of the creatures are lizards and insects such as scorpions. There are also different kinds of rats as well as other, larger animals.

You can hear the animals squeaking and growling near water holes and springs. That's where the coyotes, badgers, bobcats, foxes, and birds gather - all hunting for food and water. When the rare spring does bubble up in the desert, plants and trees begin to grow. An island of green like this is called an 'oasis'.

Many people choose to live in the desert. In late afternoon the sky turns crimson and gold, and the mountains make purple shadows. And at night the stars seem close enough to touch.

LEARN MORE! READ THESE ARTICLES...
ALGERIA (VOLUME 8) • CAMELS (VOLUME 12) • OASIS (VOLUME 1)

SEARCH LIGHT

Fill in
the gap:
Every continent
except
_____
has a desert.

This desert in California, U.S., called Death Valley, is both beautiful and dangerous. It's also the lowest point below sea level in the Western Hemisphere.
Joseph Sohm—Chromosohm/Photo Researchers

DID YOU KNOW?

Desert sands are known to 'sing'. For some reason that scientists do not yet fully understand, sand sometimes makes a booming, barking, or humming noise when walked upon or moved by some other natural force.

Fingers of Land

A peninsula is a body of land surrounded by water on three sides. The word 'peninsula' comes from the Latin *paene insula*, which means 'almost an island'. There are peninsulas on every **continent**, but each one is different. Most peninsulas of any significance extend into the sea or very large lakes.

In the United States, Florida is a peninsula. The state of Alaska qualifies as one and has several smaller peninsulas of its own.

One of the last great wilderness areas in the United States is on the Olympic Peninsula in Washington state. It is surrounded by the Pacific Ocean, the Strait of Juan de Fuca, and Puget Sound. It has a rainforest, rivers, **alpine** peaks, glaciers, and such creatures as salmon and elk.

In Mexico there are two main peninsulas, the Yucatán Peninsula in the east and Baja California in the west. The Yucatán Peninsula draws tourists to the ruins of great Mayan cities such as Uxmal and Chichén Itzá.

Another famous peninsula is the Sinai Peninsula in Egypt. It is triangular in shape. The peninsula links Africa and Asia. In Jewish history the Sinai Peninsula is known as the site where God appeared before Moses and gave him the Ten Commandments.

Europe too has several peninsulas. In northern Europe the Scandinavian Peninsula contains the countries of Norway and Sweden. Denmark forms another. And the Iberian Peninsula in southern Europe is made up of Spain and Portugal. Italy and part of Greece are peninsulas as well.

The world's largest peninsula is Arabia, at over 2.6 million square kilometres. Other important peninsulas in Asia include Korea and Southeast Asia.

LEARN MORE! READ THESE ARTICLES...
ISLANDS (VOLUME 1) • ITALY (VOLUME 6) • KOREAN PENINSULA (VOLUME 7)

DID YOU KNOW?

Peninsulas in warm climates, such as Iberia (Spain and Portugal), Italy, and Florida, tend to be popular tourist destinations owing to their miles of beaches.

SEARCH LIGHT

Which of the following are peninsulas? (Feel free to consult your classroom map or globe.)

Korea	Britain
Portugal	Arabia
Italy	Florida
Hawaii	Denmark

Answer: The only two that are *not* peninsulas are Hawaii and Britain. They are islands.

Endangered Ecosystems

Imagine a forest with a carpet of wet leaves littering the ground. If you look up, you see only a **canopy** of broad green leaves. There are wildflowers on the trees. You can hear water drops, insects, birds, and, perhaps, the distant screech of a monkey. The place you are picturing is a rainforest.

A rainforest is a kind of **ecosystem** - a community of all the living things in a region, their physical environment, and all their interrelationships.

Rainforests are dense, wet, and green because they get large amounts of rain. The Amazon Rainforest in South America is the world's largest rainforest. Other large rainforests lie in Central Africa and Southeast Asia. Northeastern Australia's 'dry rainforest' has a long dry season followed by a season of heavy rainfall.

View of the Venezuelan rainforest canopy from the air.
© Fotografia, Inc./Corbis

In a rainforest nothing is wasted. Everything is **recycled**. When leaves fall, flowers wilt, or animals die on the forest floor, they decay. This releases nutrients into the soil that become food for the roots of trees and plants. Water **evaporates** in the forest and forms clouds above the trees. Later this water falls again as rain.

Rainforests are rich in plants and animals. Many have not even been discovered yet. Some rainforest plants have given us important medicines. These include aspirin, which is a pain reliever, and curare, used to help people relax during medical operations.

Unfortunately, the rainforests are being destroyed rapidly. The trees are felled for **timber** and to clear land for farming. Animals living in these forests are facing extinction. And once lost, these animals and forests cannot be replaced.

LEARN MORE! READ THESE ARTICLES...
AMAZON: RAINFOREST RIVER (VOLUME 9) • CONGO (VOLUME 8)
MEDICINE (VOLUME 2)

DID YOU KNOW?
Rainforests are being cut down or burned at an alarming rate. Scientists estimate that every day a rainforest the size of New York City is lost.

SEARCH LIGHT

What's one important way that rainforests help people? (Hint: Think of aspirin.)

Answer: Rainforest plants have helped unlock the secrets of many of the drugs we use to keep ourselves healthy today. Aspirin is one of these.

SEARCH LIGHT

What's one way that swamps and marshes are alike? What's one way that they're different?

Grassy Wetlands

A marsh is a wetland - an area of land containing much soil moisture that does not drain well. Swamps are also wetlands. The main difference is that while trees grow in a swamp, grasses grow in a marsh. Marsh grasses have shallow roots that spread and bind mud together. This slows the flow of water, which drops rich soil deposits and encourages the growth of the marsh.

DID YOU KNOW?
The largest marsh in the world is the Florida Everglades. This marsh-swamp combination is somewhat more than 3,200 square kilometres and is home to many extraordinary animals, including the very rare Florida panther.

There are two main types of marshes - freshwater marshes and salt marshes. Freshwater marshes are found at the mouths of rivers. These marshes are famous as bird **sanctuaries**. They provide an important **habitat** for many birds, mammals, and insects. If we didn't have the marshes, then we would lose many of these animals. There simply isn't anywhere else where they can survive.

The Amazon in South America, the Congo in Africa, the Nile in Egypt, the Tigris and Euphrates in Iraq, and the Mekong in Vietnam all have large freshwater marshes.

Did you know that the rice you eat grows in freshwater marshes? Rice is the most important of all marsh plants. It provides a major portion of the world's food.

Salt marshes are formed by seawater flooding and draining flat land as tides go in and out. The grasses of a salt marsh will not grow if the ground is permanently flooded. Salt marshes are found along the east coast of the United States, in the Arctic, in the U.K., in northern Europe, in Australia, and in New Zealand.

LEARN MORE! READ THESE ARTICLES...
MOSQUITOES (VOLUME 11) • RUSHES AND REEDS (VOLUME 10)
SWAMPS (VOLUME 1)

The Ruby Marshes in the state of Nevada, U.S., provide a great example of what these grassy wetlands look like.
© David Muench/Corbis

Answer: Both swamps and marshes are wetlands and support a lot of wildlife. But while trees grow in swamps, grasses grow in marshes.

Waterlogged Forests

People once believed that drinking the tea-coloured water from the Great Dismal Swamp in the eastern coastal United States was magic. They believed it prevented illness and made people live longer. The swamp water wasn't magic, of course. But its peculiar colour, plus swampland's mysterious and exotic beauty, made an ideal setting for such folklore.

Swamps are special wetland areas found throughout the world. They are usually very wet, wide, low, and green and have many trees. Swamps are found in areas where the water doesn't drain and keeps the ground **waterlogged**. Swamps are different from marshes and other kinds of wetlands by having trees as their major form of plant life.

Freshwater swamps tend to develop in low-lying regions around rivers. The trees in a swamp lack deep-growing roots. Few kinds of plants can live in swamps. But some swamps support a variety of plants and a great number of animal species as well.

For example, giant tupelo and bald cypress trees grow in the Okefenokee Swamp of the south-eastern United States. Spanish moss, brush, and vines grow on these trees. There are exotic flowers like lilies, rare orchids, and floating hearts. Wildlife is varied and plentiful too. There are 175 species of birds and at least 40 species of mammals. These include raccoons, black bears, white-tailed deer, bobcats, foxes, and otters. Alligators also live there, as do mosquitoes, which breed in standing water.

Besides river swamps, there are saltwater and mangrove swamps. Salt swamps are formed by flooding seawater. Mangrove trees are very hardy and can survive in sandy, salty areas. The **deltas** of the Mekong, Amazon, Congo, and Ganges rivers have large mangrove swamps.

LEARN MORE! READ THESE ARTICLES...
ALLIGATORS AND CROCODILES (VOLUME 11) • MARSHES (VOLUME 1)
ORCHIDS (VOLUME 10)

The bald cypress survives well in south-eastern U.S. swamps. Its roots tend to grow out to the sides rather than just straight down. They often send woody knobs called 'knees' above the waterline. The knees may help the tree get air, and are popular household ornaments.
© David Muench/Corbis

SEARCH LIGHT

Which item from the list below does *not* describe a swamp?
a) wet all the time
b) trees as major plant life
c) lots of grasses
d) formed by rivers and salt water

Answer: c) lots of grasses. Swamps have trees rather than grasses. Marshes are wetlands where grasses are the most common plant life.

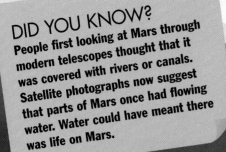

DID YOU KNOW?
People first looking at Mars through modern telescopes thought that it was covered with rivers or canals. Satellite photographs now suggest that parts of Mars once had flowing water. Water could have meant there was life on Mars.

The Power
of Flowing Water

It seems fairly obvious what rivers are for. They give us water to drink and fish to eat. They do these things for many animals too. But it might surprise you to learn that rivers have some even bigger jobs.

For one thing, rivers deliver water to lakes and oceans. Another major task is changing the face of the land, and this second job makes a huge difference. No other force changes as much of the world's surface as running water does. In fact, the world's rivers could completely **erode** the face of the Earth, though it might take them 25 million years to do it.

We can see rivers' **handiwork** all around us. Valleys are carved out when rivers slowly cut through rock and carry off soil. Canyons and gorges are young valleys.

SEARCH LIGHT

Fill in
the gap:
You could
describe one of
a river's main jobs
as being a sculptor
of _____.

Another impressive bit of river handiwork is the waterfall. Waterfalls happen when a river wears away soft rock and then drops down onto hard rock that it can't erode. Some falls are **harnessed** to produce electricity.

The world's tallest waterfall is Angel Falls in Venezuela. It drops an incredible 979 metres. Khone Falls on the Mekong River in Southeast Asia sends 9.5 million litres of water over the edge every second - the most of any falls and nearly double the flow of North America's Niagara Falls.

The world's longest river is the Nile in North Africa. The Amazon in South America is a little shorter but carries more water than any other river.

LEARN MORE! READ THESE ARTICLES...
FLOODS (VOLUME 1) • GRAND CANYON (VOLUME 9)
NILE RIVER: EGYPT'S GIFT (VOLUME 8)

Answer: You could describe one of a river's main jobs as being a sculptor of land.

Engulfed by Water

Take a small bowl and place a sponge in it. Now slowly pour water into the bowl. The sponge soaks up the water. But once the sponge is full, the bowl begins to fill up with water. If you pour more water, the bowl will overflow.

This is what happens in a flood. The ground is like a giant sponge that soaks up rainwater until it is full. Some of the water dries and goes back into the air. The rest, called 'runoff', can't be soaked up and can cause floods.

There are different types of flood. Spring floods occur when heavy winter snows melt rapidly. Floods caused by heavy rains can occur at any time of the year. Rivers overflow their banks, and the ground can't soak up the extra water.

The rain and wind accompanying hurricanes (or typhoons, in the Pacific Ocean) can also cause floods. Huge ocean waves **overwhelm** coastal towns, and the heavy rains cause rivers and streams to flood nearby areas. Hurricane-created floods struck Central America in 1998, killing more than 20,000 people and leaving one and a half million homeless.

A flash flood, however, comes without warning. When a **cloudburst** occurs in a hilly region or in a dry riverbed, the runoff is fast. The ground doesn't have time to soak up the rainwater. Destructive flash floods happen when a great deal of water overflows all at once.

Volcanic eruptions and earthquakes at sea may cause huge waves called 'tsunamis', which may swamp coasts. The volcanic eruption of Krakatoa in 1883 formed waves that flooded whole districts in Indonesia.

DID YOU KNOW?
A disastrous flood in 1919 in Boston, Massachussetts, U.S., had nothing to do with water. A molasses tank exploded, and over 7.5 million sticky litres poured out in a 4.5-metre-high wave. Twenty-one people died, and for years Boston smelled of molasses.

LEARN MORE! READ THESE ARTICLES...
PRAGUE (VOLUME 6) • TSUNAMIS (VOLUME 1) • WATER POWER (VOLUME 2)

In 1999 these people and others suffered losses in the
floods that followed Hurricane Irene in Florida, U.S.
© AFP/Corbis

SEARCH LIGHT

**Fill in
the gaps:
When it rains,
the _____
soaks up the water.
Water that doesn't get
soaked up is called
'_____'.**

**Answer: When it rains, the ground soaks up the water. Water that
doesn't get soaked up is called 'runoff'.**

33

SEARCH LIGHT

How is an oasis like an island?

In the Sahara desert an oasis like this depends heavily on date palms. They provide both food and enough shade to grow other plants that are too sensitive to grow directly in the desert sun.
Robert Everts–Stone/Getty Images

Water in the Desert

Probably the most precious thing in the world is fresh water. If a person was lost in a desert without any special equipment or supplies, he or she would soon die from lack of water.

It is therefore not surprising that very few people live in the desert. But some people do. Where do they stay? Obviously, they stay where there is water.

A place in the desert with a natural supply of fresh water is called an 'oasis'. An oasis has enough water to support a variety of plants.

Most oases (the plural of 'oasis') have underground water sources such as springs or wells. Al-Hasa is the largest oasis in the Middle Eastern country of Saudi Arabia. It has hectares and hectares of palm groves and other crops.

But not all oases have a constant supply of water. Some areas have dry channels called 'wadis', where springs sometimes flow. And desert areas at higher elevations sometimes receive extra rain to support plant life.

In the Sahara, people can live year-round in the oases because the water supply is permanent. The oases allow crops to be watered, and desert temperatures make crops grow quickly. The date palm is the main source of food. However, in its shade grow citrus fruits, figs, peaches, apricots, vegetables, and cereals such as wheat, barley, and millet.

The Siwa Oasis in western Egypt has about 200 springs. It is a very fertile oasis, and thousands of date palms and olive trees grow there. In fact, the people living in this oasis export dates and olive oil to other places in the world.

LEARN MORE! READ THESE ARTICLES…
DESERTS (VOLUME 1) • LIBYA (VOLUME 8)
PALM (VOLUME 10)

DID YOU KNOW?

Few people realize just how extreme desert weather can be. The hottest desert temperature recorded is 58°C, in Libya. And in Chile there is a desert that apparently hasn't had any rain for the last 400 years.

Answer: An oasis is like an island of water surrounded by a sea of sand. It's like a reverse island.

SEARCH LIGHT

How do
the oceans
help plants
grow?

The World of Water

Did you know that nearly three-fourths of the Earth's surface is under water? And almost all of that water is in one of the four major oceans. From biggest to smallest the oceans are: the Pacific, the Atlantic, the Indian, and the Arctic. Seas, such as the Mediterranean and the Caribbean, are divisions of the oceans.

© Kennan Ward/Corbis

The oceans are in constant motion. The **gravity** of the Moon and the Sun pulls on the oceans, causing tides - the regular rising and falling of the ocean along beaches and coastlines. The Earth's **rotation** makes the oceans circulate clockwise in the Northern **Hemisphere** and **anticlockwise** in the Southern Hemisphere. And winds cause waves to ripple across the ocean surface, as well as helping currents to flow underneath.

Currents are like rivers within the ocean. Some are warm-water currents, which can affect temperatures on land, and some are cold-water currents, which generally flow deeper. Major ocean currents, such as the Gulf Stream off the North American coast, also make for faster ocean travel.

We know less about the oceans than we do about the Moon. The ocean depths hide dramatic deep trenches and enormous mountain ranges. The Mid-Oceanic Ridge is a 65,000-kilometre range that circles the globe.

Oceans affect our lives in important ways. They provide fish to eat. They add moisture to the air to form clouds. And the clouds then make the rain that helps plants grow. Some scientists are even working on affordable ways to turn salt water into fresh water for drinking, cooking, washing, and watering crops. If they succeed, it will be one of the most important inventions of our time.

LEARN MORE! READ THESE ARTICLES…
SEAWEED (VOLUME 10) • SHIPS (VOLUME 2) • WAVES (VOLUME 1)

DID YOU KNOW?
The Mariana Trench near the island of Guam has the deepest spot measured so far, at nearly 11 kilometres. The world's highest mountain, Mount Everest, could sink in that spot and still have a mile of water above it.

Answer: Ocean water helps plants grow by adding moisture to the air, which turns into clouds. When the clouds gather enough moisture, it rains, which helps plants grow.

SEARCH LIGHT

True or false? The Atlantic is the saltiest ocean.

SOUTH AMERICA

DID YOU KNOW?

Legend says that the Atlantic Ocean hides the remains of Atlantis, an island that supposedly sank beneath the sea. People have believed stories of Atlantis for many hundreds of years and have spent almost as much time searching for it.

EUROPE

The Youngest Ocean

The Atlantic Ocean is the world's second largest ocean, after the Pacific. It covers nearly 20 per cent of the Earth. If you tasted water from all the oceans, you'd find the Atlantic to be the saltiest. And even though it is very old, it is actually the youngest ocean.

The Atlantic Ocean lies between Europe and Africa on one side of the globe and North and South America on the other. It reaches from the Arctic Ocean in the north to Antarctica in the south.

Like all oceans, the Atlantic has large movements of water **circulating** in it called 'currents'. Atlantic water currents move **clockwise** in the northern half of the world, but **anticlockwise** in the southern half. The Gulf Stream, a powerful and warm current in the North Atlantic, moves along the east coast of North America. There and elsewhere, the Gulf Stream has important effects on the weather.

Millions of tons of fish are caught each year in the waters of the Atlantic Ocean. In fact, more than half of all the fish caught in the world come from the Atlantic. The Atlantic is also used for activities such as sailing, wind surfing, and whale watching.

But despite the usefulness and magnificence of the Atlantic Ocean, the level of pollution has increased. People have allowed fertilizers, **pesticides,** and waste from toilets and sinks and factories to get into the ocean waters. As people and businesses try harder to stop pollution, the Atlantic will again become a healthier home for its animal and plant life.

LEARN MORE! READ THESE ARTICLES...
EUROPE (VOLUME 6) • MEDITERRANEAN SEA (VOLUME 1)
POLLUTION (VOLUME 1)

AFRICA

Answer: TRUE.

DID YOU KNOW?

Whales, the largest animals in the Pacific, have had a strange evolutionary journey. Their early ancestors were land mammals with legs but eventually came to live in the sea and became whales.

AUSTRALIA

SEARCH LIGHT

Fill in
the gaps:
The Pacific is the

_____

and the

_____

of all the oceans.

40

Largest Ocean in the World

NORTH AMERICA

The Pacific Ocean is the largest ocean in the world. It covers nearly one-third of the Earth. The Pacific is also deeper than any other ocean. The Pacific Ocean lies between the **continents** of Asia and Australia on the west and North and South America on the east.

The Pacific's deepest parts are the ocean trenches. These trenches are long, narrow, steep, and very deep holes at the bottom of the ocean. Of the 20 major trenches in the world, 17 are in the Pacific Ocean. The deepest trench is the Mariana Trench. It is deeper than Mount Everest (the highest mountain on land) is tall.

There are also many islands in the Pacific Ocean. Some islands were once part of the continents. Some that were part of Asia and Australia include Taiwan, the Philippines, Indonesia, Japan, and New Zealand.

Other Pacific islands have risen up from the floor of the ocean. Many of them are born from volcanoes. These islands are built over thousands of years by the lava that comes out of the volcanoes. The Hawaiian Islands and the Galapagos, for example, started as volcanoes.

The Pacific Ocean is very rich in **minerals.** It also has large supplies of oil and natural gas. And there is rich **marine** life in the Pacific. Fish such as salmon in northwestern America, bonito and prawns in Japan and Russia, and anchovy in Peru are all major food sources for people worldwide.

LEARN MORE! READ THESE ARTICLES...
ATLANTIC OCEAN (VOLUME 1) • GALAPAGOS ISLANDS (VOLUME 9)
JAPAN: VOLCANOES, EARTHQUAKES, AND PLUM RAINS (VOLUME 7)

SOUTH AMERICA

Answer: The Pacific is the largest and the deepest of all the oceans.

AFRICA

Arabian Peninsula

India

SEARCH LIGHT

Fill in the gap with the correct number: The Indian Ocean is _____ times as big as the United States.

ANTARCTICA

DID YOU KNOW?
The world's longest mountain chain is the undersea Mid-Oceanic Ridge. It stretches from the Arctic Ocean through the Atlantic and Indian oceans to the Pacific Ocean. The ridge is four times as long as the Andes, Rockies, and Himalayas *combined*!

Ocean Between Many Continents

Millions of years ago there was one huge mass of land in the Southern **Hemisphere**. It was the continent of Gondwanaland. But over many, many years Gondwanaland slowly broke up into the continents of South America, Africa, Antarctica, and Australia, as well as most of India.

The water that filled the growing space between these continents is now the Indian Ocean. The Indian Ocean is a huge body of salt water. It is the third largest ocean in the world - about five and a half times the size of the United States!

People from India, Egypt, and ancient Phoenicia (now mostly in Lebanon) were the first to explore this ocean. Later, Arabian merchants set up trade routes to the east coast of Africa. And Indian traders and priests carried their civilization into the East Indies. The dependable winds from the rainy season known as the 'monsoon' made these voyages possible.

Today the Indian Ocean has major sea routes. They connect the Middle East, Africa, and East Asia with Europe and the Americas. Ships carry tanks of **crude oil** from the oil-rich Persian Gulf and Indonesia. The oil is important to modern society, but spills from these oil tankers can endanger ocean life.

The Indian Ocean is alive with plants, as well as animals such as sponges, crabs, brittle stars, flying fish, dolphins, tuna, sharks, sea turtles, and sea snakes. Albatross, frigate birds, and several kinds of penguins also make their home there.

AUSTRALIA

LEARN MORE! READ THESE ARTICLES…
INDIA (VOLUME 7) • OIL (VOLUME 2)
PACIFIC OCEAN (VOLUME 1)

Answer: The Indian Ocean is 5½ times as big as the United States.

43

The Sea in the Middle of Land

Italy

The Mediterranean Sea gets its name from two Latin words: *medius*, meaning 'middle', and *terra*, meaning 'land'. The Mediterranean Sea is almost entirely surrounded by land. It's right between Africa, Europe, and Asia.

The Mediterranean is a bit larger than the African country of Algeria. But more important than its size is its location. Its central position made the Mediterranean an important waterway for a number of classical cultures, such as those of Italy, Greece, Egypt, and Turkey.

Many **channels** connect the Mediterranean with other bodies of water. The Strait of Gibraltar connects the Mediterranean with the Atlantic Ocean. The Dardanelles and the Bosporus connect it with the Black Sea, between Europe and Asia. And the Suez Canal is a man-made channel connecting the Mediterranean Sea with the Red Sea, which lies between the Arabian **Peninsula** and North Africa.

Three major rivers also lead into the Mediterranean Sea: the Rhône in France, the Po in Italy, and the Nile in Egypt. But the water from most of the rivers **evaporates** quickly. Instead, the Mediterranean Sea gets most of its water from the Atlantic Ocean. So Mediterranean water is very salty.

There are many popular tourist **resorts** along the Mediterranean. These include some of the Mediterranean's many islands, such as Corsica, Sardinia, Sicily, Malta, Crete, and Cyprus. Tourists often like to take a **cruise** across the Mediterranean. They get to visit many different countries all at once, try lots of different food, and see the **remains** of various ancient civilizations.

LEARN MORE! READ THESE ARTICLES...
ITALY (VOLUME 6) • NILE RIVER: EGYPT'S GIFT (VOLUME 8)
SUEZ CANAL (VOLUME 8)

AFRICA

DID YOU KNOW?

Various Mediterranean regions have special marriage customs. One area's custom is to cut the groom's tie into many pieces, which are then sold to the wedding guests for honeymoon money.

Bosporus

Dardanelles

Turkey
(ASIA)

SEARCH LIGHT

Egypt

Which ocean provides the most water to the Mediterranean?

Answer: The Atlantic Ocean supplies most of the Mediterranean's water.

The Ocean's Rise and Fall

Perhaps you have been to the beach and put your towel very close to the water. Then, when it was time to leave, the water seemed to have shrunk and was now far away from your towel.

At low tide the water slips low down on the beach. At high tide it will creep back up.
© Tim Thompson/Corbis

What actually happens is even more surprising. At high tide the water creeps up the beach. At low tide the water slips down. So the water really doesn't shrink; it simply goes away! But how, and where?

Most seashores have about two high tides and two low tides per day. It takes a little more than 6 hours for the rising waters to reach high tide. It takes another 6 hours for the falling waters to reach low tide. This 12-hour rise and fall is called the 'tidal cycle'.

Tides are caused mainly by the gravity of the Moon and the Sun pulling on the Earth. This causes ocean waters to pile up in a big bump of water directly beneath the Sun and the Moon. As the Earth **rotates**, the tidal bumps try to follow the two heavenly bodies.

The Sun and the Moon are in line with the Earth during a full moon or a new moon. Their gravity added together causes higher-than-normal high tides called 'spring tides'. When the Moon and the Sun are farthest out of line, their gravity forces offset each other. This causes lower-than-normal high tides, called 'neap tides'.

The tides in the Bay of Fundy in Canada rise higher than 16 metres. Beach towels and umbrellas at the Bay of Fundy don't stand a chance!

LEARN MORE! READ THESE ARTICLES…
GRAVITY (VOLUME 2) • MOON (VOLUME 2)
WAVES (VOLUME 1)

DID YOU KNOW?

Some narrow rivers that empty into the sea develop large waves when extremely high tides rush into them. These waves, called 'tidal bores', force the river's flow to change direction as they pass.

At high tide the water creeps high up on the beach.

SEARCH LIGHT

It takes 6 hours for the tide to rise or fall. When the tide has both risen and fallen, that makes one tidal cycle. How long does it take for two tidal cycles?

Answer: Each tidal cycle has got one rising tide and one falling tide. It takes 6 hours for the tide to rise or fall, so it takes 12 hours for it to do both. That is, 12 hours for one tidal cycle. Two tidal cycles then take 24 hours.

DID YOU KNOW?
According to researchers in Canada, the tallest ocean wave ever recorded was 34 metres high.

Movement on the Seas

The sea never seems to sit still. Its waves rise and fall. On beaches they push forward and fall back. But what makes ocean water into waves?

Most waves are created by the wind. The wind blows along the surface of the water and forces waves in the same direction. The top of a wave is called the 'crest' and the lowest part in between the crests is known as the 'trough'. When waves roll through the open ocean, they're called 'swell'. As they reach the shore, their crests get higher and closer together and finally topple over. Then they're called 'breakers' or 'surf'.

A gentle wind makes long waves that don't rise very high. But stronger winds push harder on the water and create taller waves. Big storms mean strong winds, and that means huge, powerful waves.

Major storms at sea, called 'hurricanes' or 'typhoons', can cause enormous waves. Some are so big that they can smash seaside houses into pieces, or tip over ships that get in their way. During violent storms, waves have been known to reach to the tops of lighthouses and to toss boats completely out of the water.

The most destructive waves are tsunamis, but they're quite different from other waves. Tsunamis - also wrongly called 'tidal waves' - are not caused by tides or by the wind. These huge waves are created by underwater earthquakes or volcanic eruptions.

SEARCH LIGHT

'Breakers' is another word for
a) surf.
b) trough.
c) crest.

LEARN MORE! READ THESE ARTICLES...
OCEANS (VOLUME 1) • RADIO (VOLUME 2) • TIDES (VOLUME 1)

Without waves, the very popular sport of surfing wouldn't be possible. Riding a surfboard in waves like these requires great balance, skill, and a lot of nerve!
© Rick Doyle/Corbis

Answer: a) surf.

Waves of Destruction

A powerful earthquake struck the coast of Chile in 1960. Frightened, people got into their boats and went to the harbour to escape the disaster. Soon enormous waves caused by the earthquake rose up from the sea. These violent waves were each more than three stories high. They destroyed all the boats and killed the people in them. The waves then travelled for 15 hours across the Pacific Ocean to Hilo in Hawaii, where they destroyed more property.

These waves are known as 'tsunamis', from the Japanese for 'harbour wave'.

A tsunami is a large destructive wave created by the shock from an earthquake or volcanic eruption. The impact of a **meteorite** could also create a tsunami. Tsunamis travel fast and have the force to destroy entire coastal communities within moments.

A tsunami can travel at speeds of 725 kilometres per hour or more (as fast as a jet plane) and packs tremendous force. As a tsunami approaches land, it grows larger. It continues to travel until its energy is completely used up. All low-lying coastal areas are **vulnerable** to a tsunami disaster.

In July 1998 a tsunami **devastated** the northwest coast of Papua New Guinea. It was caused by an earthquake 19 kilometres offshore that measured 7.0 on the Richter scale. (The biggest earthquakes have not reached higher than 9.0.) The tsunami swept away three coastal villages. Afterwards, nothing remained but sand.

LEARN MORE! READ THESE ARTICLES...
CYCLONES (VOLUME 1) • VOLCANOES (VOLUME 1) • WAVES (VOLUME 1)

SEARCH LIGHT

Which of these does *not* cause a tsunami?
a) earthquake
b) volcanic eruption
c) high winds

DID YOU KNOW?

When tsunamis strike land, they generally first suck all the water out of any harbours.

Answer: c) high winds

The Biggest Ice Cubes

Icebergs are simply broken-off pieces of glaciers or polar ice sheets that float out into the ocean. Very big pieces. Even little icebergs called 'growlers' are as big as buses. Big ones are longer than freight trains and as high as skyscrapers.

One especially surprising thing about an iceberg is that the part you see above the water is only a small bit of the whole iceberg. Most of the iceberg is underwater. You can see the way an iceberg floats by doing an easy experiment at home.

Fill a clear glass half full of very cold water. Drop an ice cube into the glass. Notice how most of the ice cube stays below the water.

The ice cube floats just the way an iceberg floats. And as the cube melts, it turns over, just as an iceberg does. Icebergs melt when they float away from freezing waters into warmer waters. Icebergs always start in the parts of the world where it stays cold all the time, near the North or the South Pole.

Icebergs can be very dangerous when they float, big and silent, into the path of a ship. In the past many ships were wrecked because they hit an iceberg. Fortunately, this hardly ever happens anymore. This is because most modern ships have radar that finds the icebergs before they become a problem.

In addition, special airplanes from the International Ice Patrol watch for icebergs in likely areas, and satellites scan the oceans every day. Maps and warnings are regularly sent by radio to all the ships in nearby waters.

LEARN MORE! READ THESE ARTICLES...
ECHOES (VOLUME 1) • GLACIERS (VOLUME 1) • SUBMARINES (VOLUME 2)

You can see from the size of the boat how big some icebergs actually are. But the much larger part of an iceberg is under the water!
Pal Hermansen—Stone/Getty Images

DID YOU KNOW?
On 14-15 April 1912, just before midnight, the ocean liner *Titanic* struck an iceberg and sank on its very first voyage. Only 705 people survived, and 1,522 of the passengers and crew died.

SEARCH LIGHT

Icebergs are broken-off pieces of
a) islands.
b) glaciers.
c) ice cubes.

Answer: b) glaciers.

Rivers of Ice

In high mountains there are places that are packed full of ice. These ice packs are called 'glaciers' and look like giant frozen rivers. And like rivers, glaciers flow - but usually so slowly you can't see them move.

It takes a long time to make a glacier. First, snow falls on the mountains. It collects year after year, until there is a thick layer called a 'snowfield'.

In summer the surface of the snowfield melts and sinks into the snow below it. There it freezes and forms a layer of ice. This too happens year after year, until most of the snowfield has been changed into ice. The snowfield is now a glacier.

The snow and ice in a glacier can become very thick and heavy. The glacier then begins to actually move under its own weight and creeps down the mountain valley. It has now become a valley glacier.

The valley glacier moves slowly but with enormous force. As it moves, it scrapes the sides of the mountain and tears off pieces of it. Sometimes it tears off chunks as big as a house. As the glacier moves down the mountain into warmer regions, the ice begins to melt. The icy water fills rivers and streams.

Many thousands of years ago, much of the Earth's surface was covered with moving glaciers. This period is sometimes called the Ice Age. As the world warmed, most of the ice melted away and formed many of the rivers, lakes, and seas around us today - including the Great Lakes in North America, which have an area greater than the entire United Kingdom.

LEARN MORE! READ THESE ARTICLES…
ICEBERGS (VOLUME 1) • NORWAY (VOLUME 6) • RIVERS (VOLUME 1)

A valley glacier is
a) a glacier that has grown up in a valley.
b) a thick layer of snow.
c) a glacier that has started to move down a mountain.

In Alaska's Glacier Bay National Park, the 16 glaciers that descend from the mountains present an amazing sight.
© Neil Rabinowitz/Corbis

Answer: c) a glacier that has started to move down a mountain.

Floating Water

Have you ever looked up at the clouds and wondered what they're made of?

Well, they're made of water - thousands of litres of water, floating high in the sky.

It's easier to believe this when you know that cloud water takes the form of tiny droplets. The droplets are so tiny that you couldn't see one if it was separated from all the others.

Sometimes the water droplets join together around tiny pieces of dust in the air. These droplets become bigger and bigger as more of them collect. When they become too heavy to float, they fall - 'plop!' That's rain!

There are three main kinds of cloud. 'Cumulus' are the small puffballs or great woolly-looking clouds that are flat on the bottom. 'Stratus' are low clouds, usually streaky or without much shape. And 'cirrus' are light feathery clouds, like the ones in the photo. Sometimes, when a cirrus cloud is high in the very cold air, the whole cloud is made of ice.

Adding 'nimbus' to any of these names changes it to mean a rain cloud. Tall white cottony rain clouds are called 'cumulonimbus', or thunderclouds. They often bring thunderstorms. Flat grey rain clouds are called 'nimbostratus'. They usually bring only rain.

Snow, **sleet**, and **hail** also fall from clouds. Snow and sleet usually fall on cold winter days. Hailstones can fall even on a warm summer day.

And you may not realize it, but you've probably been right inside a cloud yourself. A cloud so close to the ground that we can walk through it is 'fog'.

LEARN MORE! READ THESE ARTICLES...
ACID RAIN (VOLUME 1)
LIQUIDS, SOLIDS, AND GASES (VOLUME 2)
NEW ZEALAND (VOLUME 7)

SEARCH LIGHT

Which of the following describes a cumulonimbus cloud?
a) cloud on the ground
b) sleet cloud
c) fog
d) thundercloud

DID YOU KNOW?
Being on 'cloud nine' means you are feeling especially good, flying high. One explanation for the term comes from the military, where cloud types were numbered. Type nine was a tall thundercloud, and jets would have to fly very high to get over one.

Nature's Fireworks

It can be fun playing in gentle rain, splashing in puddles and chasing raindrops. But this would be a dangerous thing to do if there were thunderclouds above.

Thunderclouds are the large, dark, often fast-moving clouds that come out during storms. Thunderclouds rumble mightily during storms, and that rumbling indicates the presence of lightning. The rumbling is the sound lightning makes as it arcs across the sky.

During a thunderstorm, electricity collects in the clouds. And often this electricity is released as lightning. It's dangerous to be outside when there is a risk of lightning because it can quite easily kill someone from miles away. People have died from lightning strikes even though the storm the lightning has come from was barely visible on the **horizon**.

Lightning bolts frequently race to the ground, drawn by objects such as trees and lampposts, which are especially good conductors of electricity. Lightning is most attracted to tall objects, which is why trees, buildings, and radio towers are often struck.

Actually there are two parts to a lightning strike. The bolt from the sky is the part we don't see, because it is so fast and faint. The part we do see is the return strike. This is a bright flash of lightning that jumps up out of the ground to meet the lightning coming down and then races up to the base of the clouds.

Lightning can hurt or kill people who are struck by it. If you ever are caught in a thunderstorm, go indoors quickly or get into a car. Lightning that hits a car travels harmlessly into the ground.

DID YOU KNOW?
Florida is known as the 'lightning capital of the world'. Every year, lightning strikes in Florida more often than in any other state in the United States. Also lightning kills more people in Florida than in any other state.

LEARN MORE! READ THESE ARTICLES...
CLOUDS (VOLUME 1) • ELECTRICITY (VOLUME 2)
VICTORIA FALLS (VOLUME 8)

© A & J Verkaik/Corbis

Answer: FALSE. A tree is likely to be struck by lightning in a storm. It's better to get inside a car or a house, which will protect you even if the lightning strikes.

SEARCH LIGHT

Fill in
the gap:
The quietest
part of a cyclone
is the _____,
where there are
no winds or clouds.

Nature's Fury

A cyclone is a **rotating** storm that can be hundreds of kilometres wide. These storms can be very destructive. The winds in a cyclone usually blow at more than 120 kilometres per hour.

When a cyclone starts in the warmer waters of the Atlantic Ocean, it is called a 'hurricane'. In the western Pacific Ocean, it is known as a 'typhoon'.

From above, a cyclone looks like a huge spinning doughnut of clouds. The centre of the storm, the doughnut hole, is called the 'eye'. The eye is quiet and cloudless. When the eye passes overhead, it might seem like the storm has ended. But within an hour or two, the eye passes and the other side of the storm hits.

With its strong winds a cyclone also brings flooding rains and sometimes very high ocean waves. When a cyclone hits land, it causes severe damage. The combination of wind, rain, and waves can knock down trees, flatten houses, and wash away roads.

Most cyclones start over **tropical** oceans because areas of warm water are their source of energy. Strong rotating winds that start on land are called a 'tornado'. A tornado, such as the one pictured here, starts for different reasons and is smaller than a cyclone. But a tornado also has very strong winds, so it too can be very destructive. It can knock a train off its track or lift a house straight into the air. Fortunately, tornadoes usually die soon after they start.

LEARN MORE! READ THESE ARTICLES...
FLOODS (VOLUME 1) • PHILIPPINES (VOLUME 7) • WAVES (VOLUME 1)

Paul and LindaMarie Ambrose/Taxi/Getty Images

DID YOU KNOW?
The best way for scientists to learn a cyclone's size and strength is to fly a plane through it. That's the surest way - but certainly not the safest!

Answer: The quietest part of a cyclone is the eye, where there are no winds or clouds.

Arcs of Colour

If you've ever looked at a rainbow and wondered how all those bright colours got into the sky, you're not alone.

The ancient Greeks thought these **arcs** of colour were signs from the gods to warn people that terrible wars or storms were going to happen. The Norse people believed a rainbow was a bridge the gods used to walk down from the sky to the Earth. Other legends said there was a pot of gold waiting at the end of a rainbow.

But as beautiful as rainbows are, they aren't magic. And they aren't solid enough to walk on. In fact, a rainbow is just coloured light. The seven colours are always the same and appear in the same order: red, orange, yellow, green, blue, indigo (a very deep blue), and violet. The name 'Roy G. Biv' helps you remember the first letters and the order of the colours.

Rainbows often appear after or at the end of a storm - when the Sun is shining again but there is still some rain in the air. The sunlight looks white, but all seven rainbow colours are mixed together in it. So when a beam of sunlight passes through the raindrops, it's broken into the seven different colours.

But you don't have to wait for rain to see rainbows. They can show up in the spray of a fountain or a waterfall, or you can make your own with a hosepipe. Set the nozzle to create a spray, aim it away from the Sun, and then stand between the Sun and the spray. You've got an instant rainbow!

SEARCH LIGHT

How can the name 'Roy G. Biv' help you remember the colours of the rainbow?

DID YOU KNOW?

Contrary to some legends, there really is no 'end' of a rainbow. Rainbows are actually full circles. But because we can see only a limited distance, to the horizon of Earth and sky, we see only part of the circle.

LEARN MORE! READ THESE ARTICLES...
SIR ISAAC NEWTON (VOLUME 4)
NIAGARA FALLS (VOLUME 9)
THUNDER AND LIGHTNING (VOLUME 1)

Answer: The name gives you the first letter of each of the colours of the rainbow, in the order that they occur in the rainbow. Like this: Red Orange Yellow Green Blue Indigo Violet.

DID YOU KNOW?
People used to think that tiny spider webs in the grass were actually the beds of fairies. This is because the webs, covered with dew, looked like magic nets.

Diamond Drops of Water

SEARCH LIGHT

How does warm air make dew?

Susan and her mother had come to the park for an early morning walk. The weather had been nice and warm recently. The nights were still and there was hardly a cloud in the sky.

The park's grass glittered and winked. 'Are those diamonds?' Susan asked. It looked as if someone had sprinkled tiny diamonds all across the grass during the night.

© W. Perry Conway/Corbis

Susan bent down to touch one of the glittering points. 'It's water!' she cried out in surprise. 'How did it get here? Did it rain last night?'

'No, this isn't rainwater. It's dew.'

'What's dew?' Susan was eager to know.

'It came from the air. All air has got some water in it, you know,' said Mum.

'But I don't see any water in the air,' said Susan, looking around.

'No, of course you don't. It's in the form of **vapour**, like fog, only very light,' said Mum.

'So how does the water get onto the grass?'

'You know that steam turns into water again if it touches something cold, right?' Susan nodded. 'Well, on certain nights the air is warm and full of moisture,' Mum continued, 'but the grass and the ground are cool. So when the vapour in the warm air touches these cooler surfaces...'

'...it changes to water drops on the grass,' finished Susan. 'That must be why sometimes in the morning our car is covered with tiny drops of water.'

'That's right,' Mum smiled. 'Now let's get going on that walk!'

LEARN MORE! READ THESE ARTICLES...
CLOUDS (VOLUME 1) • KOALAS (VOLUME 12)
LIQUIDS, SOLIDS, AND GASES (VOLUME 2)

Answer: When warm air touches the cool ground, the water in the air turns into drops of dew.

SEARCH LIGHT

Find and correct the mistake: Leaves turn red if they contain a lot of carbon dioxide when the sun shines on them.

The Science of Their Changing Colours

Trees that shed their leaves every year are called 'deciduous' trees. New leaves grow again in spring.

Scientists think that plants get rid of things they can't use any more. After a flower has helped to make seeds for a plant, its petals fall off. And soon after leaves have lost their green material, called 'chlorophyll', they also fall off.

The chlorophyll in leaves uses sunlight to make sugar out of water and carbon dioxide, a gas in the air. Plants need carbon dioxide to live and grow. When leaves use carbon dioxide, another gas called 'oxygen' is produced. Plants don't need all the oxygen they produce, so they let most of it go.

Animals and humans need oxygen to live. Their bodies use oxygen, and what do you think they produce? Yes, carbon dioxide. When animals and humans breathe out, they let the carbon dioxide go.

It's easy to see that plants, animals, and humans help each other in this way.

In countries where the weather cools down in autumn, plants lose their chlorophyll, and their leaves may turn yellow or red. The yellow colour was in the leaves all summer, but there was so much green in the leaves that the yellow was hidden.

Yellow leaves turn red only if they have lots of sugar in their sap and the sun shines on them. The more sugar a leaf has, the redder it becomes. If a leaf is kept in the shade, it will stay yellow, even if it has a lot of sugar.

DID YOU KNOW?
Deciduous forests are one of the world's six major life zones: the often frozen tundra, the mostly evergreen taiga, temperate (mild) deciduous forest, tropical rainforest, grassland and savanna, and desert.

LEARN MORE! READ THESE ARTICLES...
CHAMELEON (VOLUME 11) • ENERGY (VOLUME 2)
MAPLE (VOLUME 10)

Answer: Leaves turn red if they contain a lot of sugar when the sun shines on them.

67

Sounds That See
in the Dark

'Hel-l-o-o-o-o-o!'

A boy hears an echo coming from the hills.

'Echo, talk to me,' he calls.

'...to me,' repeats the echo. '...to me...to me...to me.'

What is an echo? It's a sound you make that bounces back to you from hills or other surfaces. But how can a sound bounce? It's not a ball.

Actually, sound is a wave in the air. If you could see air in the same way as water, you'd see the waves that sounds make. Sound waves bounce only if they hit something big and solid like the side of a hill or the walls of a cave.

What if nothing stops the sound waves? Then they just get smaller and smaller. Or they are absorbed by soft things such as carpets, curtains, or large pieces of furniture. That's why we don't usually hear echoes in the house.

DID YOU KNOW?

It is said that a duck's quack is the only sound that doesn't echo. If you happen to have a duck and a long hallway, you could test this theory yourself.

Did you know that echoes can help some animals 'see' in the dark?

In pitch-black caves bats fly easily, never bumping into anything, and even catching tiny insects in the air. As they fly they make tiny whistle-like sounds. These sounds bounce back to them. The direction of the echo and the time it takes for it to return tell the bats exactly where things are as they fly.

Human beings have learned to harness echoes for navigation, too. Submarines travelling underwater use sonar to bounce sounds off of solid objects so that they can tell where those objects are located - like undersea bats!

LEARN MORE! READ THESE ARTICLES…
BATS (VOLUME 12) • RADIO (VOLUME 2) • SUBMARINES (VOLUME 2)

SEARCH LIGHT

Which
animal
uses sound
to 'see'?

Answer: Bats use echoes to tell what is around them in the dark.
Dolphins do the same thing underwater.

Killer Downpour

Rain seems to make things cleaner, doesn't it? Rain helps flowers grow and helps keep plants green. It washes the dust off cars and houses. It makes roads look shiny and it leaves a fresh smell in the air.

Scientist testing polluted lake water containing melted acid snow.
© Ted Spiegel/Corbis

But rain can be dirty. That's because, as the rain falls, it gathers up any **pollution** that's in the air. It can leave cars looking streaky and windows looking spotty.

Some rain will even ruin the paint on cars. It will damage or kill the plants it falls on and the fish living in lakes that are fed by rain. Such rain is called 'acid rain'.

This is what happens. We burn fuels such as coal, gas, and oil in our factories. This releases gases containing **elements** such as sulphur, carbon, and nitrogen into the air. These combine with moisture in the air to form such damaging substances as sulphuric acid, carbonic acid, and nitric acid. When it rains, these acids fall to earth with the water.

Acid doesn't fall to earth only in the form of rain. It can also fall as snow, sleet, and hail. It can even be in fog.

Acid rain harms many forms of life, including human life. It also damages buildings. The acid eats through stone, metal, and concrete. Acid rain has damaged some of the world's great monuments, including the **cathedrals** of Europe, the Colosseum in Rome, and the Taj Mahal in India.

LEARN MORE! READ THESE ARTICLES…
LIQUIDS, SOLIDS, AND GASES (VOLUME 2) • POLLUTION (VOLUME 1)
TAJ MAHAL (VOLUME 7)

SEARCH LIGHT

Acid rain can cause
a) water to become polluted.
b) fish to die.
c) damage to buildings.
d) plants to die.
e) all of the above.

**The unhealthy branch on the left shows the damage
that acid rain can do to plants.**
© Ted Spiegel/Corbis

DID YOU KNOW?
Acid rain destroys trees. We need trees to make oxygen and to get rid of carbon dioxide, which can be poisonous to us. Just a quarter of a hectare of trees gets rid of 2.2 tonnes of carbon dioxide a year.

DID YOU KNOW?
It's estimated that the energy saved by recycling just one glass bottle would light up a light bulb for four hours.

Harming Our Environment

Have you ever seen black smoke pouring out of factory chimneys, turning the sky a dirty grey colour? This is air pollution. Cars, lorries, buses, and even lawnmowers release gases and particles that pollute the air too. Smoke from fires and barbeques also pollutes the air.

Land pollution, water pollution, and even noise pollution are also big problems. Factories and ordinary people may thoughtlessly dump rubbish and **waste** on land or in water. And when farm chemicals that kill insect pests or help crops grow sink into the ground and water, they pollute too. And noise pollution is created by loud machines and honking horns.

Ocean life isn't safe from pollution. The picture you see here shows a crew cleaning up a polluted seashore after an oil spill. Ships carrying petroleum sometimes have accidents, and their oil spills into the ocean.

Dirty air, land, and water are dangerous. Dirty air, or **smog**, is hard to breathe and makes people and animals sick. Dirty water makes people and animals sick when they drink it or wash or live in it. It also kills plants. If land takes in too much waste, nothing will grow on it and it becomes unfit to live on.

Stopping pollution isn't easy. Most people find it hard to change the way they live, even if they want to. And governments and big companies find it even harder to change, since the changes are often unpopular or expensive.

Even small changes help, however. Reusing things instead of throwing them away helps. Using less water every day helps. So does **recycling**. And perhaps in the future people will use cleaner forms of energy, such as wind power and solar energy.

LEARN MORE! READ THESE ARTICLES…
ACID RAIN (VOLUME 1) • AUTOMOBILES (VOLUME 2)
WIND POWER (VOLUME 2)

SEARCH LIGHT

Match each item to the kind of pollution it creates.

litter   air
smog   land
oil spill   noise
car honking   water

**Answer: litter = land
smog = air
oil spill = water
car honking = noise**

To most of us, this landscape is beautiful. But to a geologist, it also tells the story of millions of years of the Earth's history.
© Layne Kennedy/Corbis

Studying the Earth

How did the Earth get its shape?

What was the world like millions of years ago?

What is the Earth made of?

Why do earthquakes happen?

These are some of the many questions that geologists try to answer. Geologists are people who study the Earth's structure and its history. The word 'geology' comes from Greek words meaning 'earth science'.

Geology is an important science. Geologists help people find useful fossil fuels, such as oil and coal, which lie hidden in the Earth's crust. Geologists also help find out where earthquakes are likely to happen. This helps people choose the safest place to put up buildings.

Because there are so many things about the Earth that geologists study, geology is divided into many separate areas. For instance, the study of physical geology looks at the changes that take place inside the Earth and the reasons for those changes. Geochemistry is concerned with the chemical **elements** that make up rocks, soil, and **minerals**. Petrology deals with rocks themselves.

Did you know that palaeontology is a form of geology? Palaeontologists study life forms that existed on Earth millions of years ago, from the tiniest **bacteria** to enormous dinosaurs. But because these creatures died so many millions of years ago, their bodies have turned into fossils - living things preserved as rock.

LEARN MORE! READ THESE ARTICLES…
GEOGRAPHY (VOLUME 1) • OIL (VOLUME 2)
ROCKS AND MINERALS (VOLUME 1)

SEARCH LIGHT

Match the scientist with what she studies:

geologist	Earth
petrologist	fossils
geochemist	rocks
palaeontologist	chemicals in rocks

The Earth's Building Blocks

You might think that rocks are fairly dull. But rocks tell the history of the Earth, including stories of giant explosions, mountains rising from the sea, and buried forests turning to stone.

Most rocks are combinations of one or more **minerals**. Minerals are inorganic, which means they are not made by living things. Yet they are extremely important to all living things. Some minerals are metals, such as iron and gold. Others are non-metallic, like quartz and calcite.

Some rocks contain the hardened **remains** of animals and plants. Limestone rock is usually made up mostly of bits and pieces of fossil shells and skeletons of sea creatures.

Sandstone canyon.
© Scott T. Smith/Corbis

All rocks fall into one of three groups, depending on how they are formed.

Igneous rocks are formed from cooling magma, which is the lava released in a volcanic eruption. The earliest rocks on Earth were igneous.

But rocks don't stay the same forever. They break down into small pieces because of the effects of wind, water, and ice. And when small pieces of rock settle together, they're known as 'sediment'. As layers of sediment settle on top of each other over many years, their weight squeezes the pieces together into solid sedimentary rock. Both photos show the very common sedimentary rock called 'sandstone', which is cemented sand.

The third group of rocks gets its name from the word 'metamorphosis', which means 'change'. Metamorphic rocks are created when extreme temperatures or pressures cause changes in igneous or sedimentary rocks. Marble is a metamorphic rock formed from intensely squeezed and heated limestone. And limestone, you'll remember, began as seashells and skeletons. This is another amazing Earth story told by a rock!

LEARN MORE! READ THESE ARTICLES...
FOSSILS (VOLUME 1) • GRAND CANYON (VOLUME 9)
TAJ MAHAL (VOLUME 7)

DID YOU KNOW?

Gold is the most easily shaped of all metals. It can be hammered until it is just 1 ten thousandth of a millimetre thick. And 30 grams of gold can be drawn into a wire more than 64 kilometres long.

Sandstone is fairly easily worn away by rushing water. Here you see a deep, narrow sandstone formation called a 'slot canyon'.
© David Muench/Corbis

SEARCH LIGHT

Minerals are inorganic, which means they are not _____.

DID YOU KNOW?
Here's a good rhyming way to remember which formation is a stalactite and which is a stalagmite. Stalactites hold 'tight' to the ceiling. Stalagmites 'might' reach the roof.

When Water Is Stronger than Stone

Caves are natural openings in the Earth large enough for a person to get in. Most have been made when rainwater or streams have worn away rock - usually a softer rock such as limestone. The wearing-away process is called 'erosion'.

Slowly, over millions of years, the water works away at the soft rock, making a small tunnel-like opening. As more and more rock wears away, the opening grows wider and deeper. Soon even more water can flow in. In time, many of these openings become huge caves, or caverns.

Mammoth Cave-Flint Ridge in Kentucky, U.S., is a linked system of caverns. It is 555 kilometres long, one of the longest in the world. In France the Jean Bernard, though much shorter (17.9 kilometres long), is one of the world's deepest caves, reaching down more than 1,535 metres.

Some caves have beautiful craggy formations called 'stalactites', like those pictured here, that hang from the cave's roof. These are made by water seeping into the cave. Each drop leaves a very tiny bit of dissolved rock on the ceiling of the cave. After thousands and thousands of years, an icicle-shaped stalactite forms.

When water drips to the cave's floor, it deposits small **particles** of solids. These slowly build up into a stalagmite, which looks like an upside-down icicle.

There are other kinds of caves that are made in different ways. When lava flows out of a volcano, it sometimes leaves gaps, making volcanic caves. When ice melts inside a glacier, glacier caves result. And ocean waves pounding on the shore year after year can wear away a cave in the face of a cliff.

SEARCH LIGHT

Which of the following is *not* a way that caves are formed?
ocean waves
lava
lightning
water erosion
ice melts

LEARN MORE! READ THESE ARTICLES...
BATS (VOLUME 12) • GLACIERS (VOLUME 1)
ROCKS AND MINERALS (VOLUME 1)

Answer: Caves aren't formed by lightning.

The Hardest-Working Gemstones in the World

Diamonds were made millions and millions of years ago when fuming volcanoes melted the **element** called 'carbon' inside some rocks. Gigantic masses of earth pressed the carbon tightly. The hot melted carbon was squeezed so tightly that by the time it cooled, it had changed into the hard **gemstones** called 'diamonds'.

Diamond jewellery.
© Lynn Goldsmith/Corbis

Some diamonds are found in the gravel and sand near rivers. Others are left in mountains by **glaciers**. Most diamonds are mined from rocks deep underground, mostly in Africa. The country of South Africa is the major source of diamonds used in jewellery.

Diamonds usually look like pieces of glass or dull stones when they're first taken out of the ground. They must be cut and shaped to be used in jewellery. And diamonds are so hard that nothing can cut them except another diamond.

Using diamond-edged tools, the diamond cutter carefully shapes and polishes the diamond so that it has straight edges and smooth surfaces. These edges and surfaces help the diamond reflect light so that it sparkles and flashes with tiny bursts of colour.

Diamonds often seem to flash like white fire. But there are diamonds that have other colours. Red, blue, and green diamonds are difficult to find. Yellow, orange, and violet diamonds are more common. Sometimes people even find black diamonds.

Only the clearest diamonds become glittering gems. But because of their hardness, even dull-looking diamonds are still valuable as cutting tools. These are called '**industrial diamonds**'. Only about 25 per cent of all diamonds are fine enough to become jewels, so most of the world's diamonds are the hard-working industrial ones.

LEARN MORE! READ THESE ARTICLES…
GEOLOGY (VOLUME 1) • ROCKS AND MINERALS (VOLUME 1)
SOUTH AFRICA: DIAMOND COUNTRY (VOLUME 8)

SEARCH LIGHT

Fill in the gap: Diamonds are so hard that only

_____

can cut them.

Raw diamonds look like chunks of glass when they're first found.
© Dave G. Houser/Corbis

Answer: Diamonds are so hard that only another diamond can cut them.

DID YOU KNOW?
Much of the chalk on Earth dates from 66 million to 144 million years ago. So much chalk comes from this time, in fact, that the whole period was named the Cretaceous Period, from the Latin word for 'chalk'.

The Remains of Tiny Shells

The material we call 'chalk' was formed during the time when dinosaurs lived on Earth. At that time the oceans were rising higher and higher until finally they covered most of the land.

Billions of tiny animals lived in those oceans. They were so small you could not have seen them - they were even smaller than the full stop at the end of this sentence. These tiny creatures had shells made from the **element** calcium. When they died, their shells fell to the bottom of the sea. After thousands of years, there were many layers of shells on the ocean floor.

As more and more of the tiny shells pressed down from the top, those on the bottom became harder and began to stick together. Eventually the shells changed into a **mineral** called 'calcite', the main ingredient of the rock known as 'limestone'.

Drawing chalk, an entirely different material from natural chalk.
© Michael T. Sedam/Corbis

Many millions of years passed after the first chalk was made. The Earth's surface changed its shape, and the land and sea developed new coastlines. This left many chalk layers on dry land, both in the middle of **continents** and by the sea. In the south of England there are chalk cliffs 244 metres high. These are the famous White Cliffs of Dover, and they are almost solid chalk!

If you had a piece of chalk from those cliffs, you could use it to write on a chalkboard. But the chalk that is used in classrooms is not dug from the cliffs or the ground. It is made in factories by mixing several different materials together.

LEARN MORE! READ THESE ARTICLES…
CORAL (VOLUME 11) • ENGLISH CHANNEL (VOLUME 6)
ROCKS AND MINERALS (VOLUME 1)

The fabulous White Cliffs of Dover in England are made up of chalk millions of years old.
© Bob Krist/Corbis

Answer: Many shells have to pile up to be heavy enough to press the bottom ones together and change them into stone.

83

Ancient Life in Stone

Would you like to see something that lived millions of years ago? You can if you find a fossil.

The **remains** or traces of plants, animals, and even **bacteria** that are preserved in stone are called 'fossils'. If you've ever pressed a coin into some clay and then removed it, you've seen the sort of image that's found in many fossils. The original thing isn't there anymore, but there's an **impression** of it left in the stone.

Fossilized fern.
© Wolfgang Kaehler/Corbis

Many fossils are easy to recognize as the living things they once were. The plant fossil in the smaller photo here, for example, looks like a tracing of a fern leaf.

Usually the harder portions of an **organism** are the parts that last long enough to turn into fossils. Sometimes the hard structures are preserved almost whole. For instance, entire fossilized dinosaur bones have been petrified, or changed into a stony substance.

Fossils are not always easy to find. Only a small fraction of all ancient life ever turned into fossils. And the fossils that did form are often buried deep underground.

You can tell that the fossils in the big photo used to be fish. However, they died millions of years ago. They sank to the riverbed and were covered with soft mud. Their flesh wasted away but their bones were held together by the mud.

Eventually the river dried up. It was filled with dust and dirt blown by the wind. The bones of the fish stayed where they were. Slowly, the mud from the riverbed turned to stone.

Finally, someone found this fossil while digging where the river used to be.

LEARN MORE! READ THESE ARTICLES...
CHARLES DARWIN (VOLUME 4)
DINOSAURS: GIANTS OF THE PAST (VOLUME 1)
OIL (VOLUME 2)

SEARCH LIGHT

It's unusual to see an animal fossil that shows more than just the bones. Why do you think bones are usually the best-preserved parts?

This fossil shows a rare picture of life in action millions of years ago. Look carefully and you can see that a big fish was eating a smaller one when they both died.
© Layne Kennedy/Corbis

DID YOU KNOW?

Over millions of years, many plant and animal remains have turned into the coal, oil, and natural gas we use for fuel. These underground energy sources are known as 'fossil fuels'.

Answer: It takes a long time for a fossil to form. Bones last much longer than flesh and organs do. So only the bones are left by the time the animal turns into a fossil.

Mammoths
and mastodons
are related to
a) horses.
b) elephants.
c) dinosaurs.

This woolly mammoth was created as part of a
museum exhibit. But primitive artists first painted
these creatures on the walls of caves.

© Jonathan Blair/Corbis

Ancient Elephants

Believe it or not, thousands of years ago some elephants wore heavy fur coats.

Actually, the mammoth was an ancestor of the modern elephant. And mastodons were distant relatives of the mammoth. Neither of these animals is around today. But at one time they roamed the Earth in great numbers.

We know a lot about these ancient creatures because scientists have found many frozen mammoth bodies, especially in the icy area of Russia known as Siberia. Both beasts largely died out at the end of the last Ice Age, about 10,000 years ago. The mammoth didn't show up until about 1 1/2 million years ago.

Mastodons and mammoths were a lot alike, but mastodons were on the planet first. They appeared about 20 million years ago. They were smaller than mammoths and had thick legs like pillars. Mastodons were covered with long reddish brown hair.

Mammoths were the size of modern elephants. The woolly mammoth had a thick furry yellowish brown undercoat with longer bristly hair over it. Like the mastodon, the mammoth had small ears and very long tusks. Despite these dangerous tusks, both animals ate only grass and other plants. The tusks may have been for shovelling snow and ice to uncover food.

Mastodons and mammoths were around at the same time as early humans. The people of the day hunted the animals, but hunting didn't make them die out. Scientists think that the mastodon and the mammoth vanished because the **glaciers** of the Ice Age destroyed much of the vegetation they relied on as food.

LEARN MORE! READ THESE ARTICLES…
ELEPHANTS (VOLUME 12) • FOSSILS (VOLUME 1)
GLACIERS (VOLUME 1)

> **DID YOU KNOW?**
> In 1816, when coal-gas lights were introduced, one of the first museum exhibits to be lit with the new invention was a mastodon skeleton.

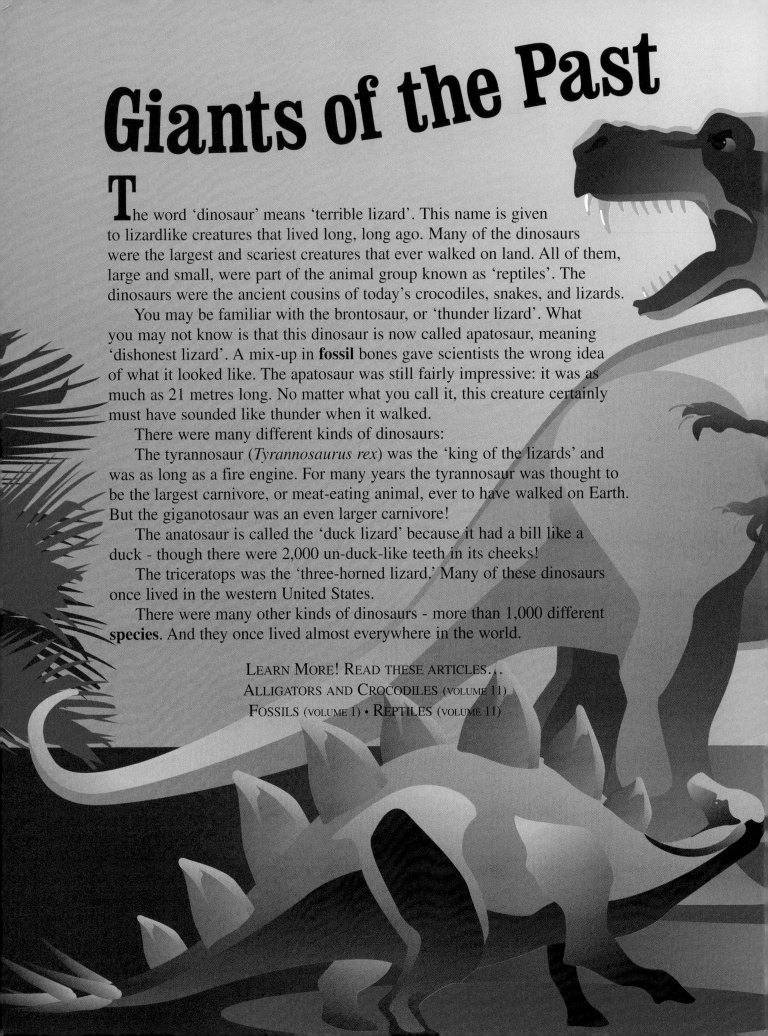

Giants of the Past

The word 'dinosaur' means 'terrible lizard'. This name is given to lizardlike creatures that lived long, long ago. Many of the dinosaurs were the largest and scariest creatures that ever walked on land. All of them, large and small, were part of the animal group known as 'reptiles'. The dinosaurs were the ancient cousins of today's crocodiles, snakes, and lizards.

You may be familiar with the brontosaur, or 'thunder lizard'. What you may not know is that this dinosaur is now called apatosaur, meaning 'dishonest lizard'. A mix-up in **fossil** bones gave scientists the wrong idea of what it looked like. The apatosaur was still fairly impressive: it was as much as 21 metres long. No matter what you call it, this creature certainly must have sounded like thunder when it walked.

There were many different kinds of dinosaurs:

The tyrannosaur (*Tyrannosaurus rex*) was the 'king of the lizards' and was as long as a fire engine. For many years the tyrannosaur was thought to be the largest carnivore, or meat-eating animal, ever to have walked on Earth. But the giganotosaur was an even larger carnivore!

The anatosaur is called the 'duck lizard' because it had a bill like a duck - though there were 2,000 un-duck-like teeth in its cheeks!

The triceratops was the 'three-horned lizard.' Many of these dinosaurs once lived in the western United States.

There were many other kinds of dinosaurs - more than 1,000 different **species**. And they once lived almost everywhere in the world.

LEARN MORE! READ THESE ARTICLES...
ALLIGATORS AND CROCODILES (VOLUME 11)
FOSSILS (VOLUME 1) • REPTILES (VOLUME 11)

DID YOU KNOW?
If you hold up your hand, you'll be looking at something still smaller than a tyrannosaur tooth.

SEARCH LIGHT

Find and correct the error in the following sentence: The apatosaur's name means 'dishonest lizard', referring to the beast's habit of robbing its neighbours.

Answer: The apatosaur's name means 'dishonest lizard', referring to the mix-up in fossils that confused scientists.

DID YOU KNOW?
Scientists think that some dinosaurs swallowed rocks, just as some birds do, to help break up food in their stomachs.

A Mystery Disappearance

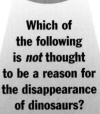

Many of the dinosaurs that once roamed the Earth were so big and strong that they didn't need to be afraid of any living thing. So why are there no dinosaurs today?

Some scientists think that when new kinds of plants began to grow on Earth, dinosaurs couldn't eat them. New kinds of animals smaller than dinosaurs also appeared during this time. They may have been able to survive better than the dinosaurs. It's also possible that disease killed them by the millions.

Not all scientists think that all dinosaurs died at once. Another explanation is that a changing **climate** killed them. We know that when they were living, the weather began to change. Summers grew shorter and winters grew colder. In some places, heat waves dried up rivers and swamps. Elsewhere, new lakes and rivers appeared, and many places were flooded. Some dinosaurs may have died because it gradually became too cold or too hot for them.

Many scientists believe that dinosaurs died because an **asteroid** struck the Earth about 65 million years ago. The dust raised by the impact would have blocked out sunlight for months, so that plants stopped growing and the temperature dropped. As a result, plant-eating dinosaurs would have died from lack of food, as would the meat eaters that hunted them.

Some scientists think that many dinosaurs **evolved** into birds. So the next time you see a robin, consider that you may be looking at a dinosaur's relative.

LEARN MORE! READ THESE ARTICLES…
ASTEROIDS (VOLUME 2) • DINOSAURS: GIANTS OF THE PAST (VOLUME 1)
LIZARDS (VOLUME 11)

Dinosaur tracks remain, but scientists still don't know what happened to the giant creatures that made them.
© Tom Bean/Corbis

The Tyrant King

It was longer than a bus, weighed more than 3.6 tonnes, and had teeth up to 30 centimetres long. The tyrannosaur may have died out 65 million years ago, but it is still one of the largest meat-eating land animals that ever lived. It's no wonder that the first scientist who discovered this frightening creature's bones called it *Tyrannosaurus rex*: '**tyrant** lizard king'.

Dinosaurs were not true lizards. However, when scientists first discovered tyrannosaur **fossils**, they did believe that such a dangerous-looking animal would have been a powerful and cruel bully amongst the dinosaurs. The tyrannosaur's jagged teeth and huge jaws make it clear that the tyrannosaur was a powerful carnivore, or meat eater.

Tyrannosaurs lived mainly in what is now North America and Asia. The creature was about 12 metres long from its head to its thick and heavy tail. The tyrannosaur probably stooped forward, with the big tail balancing its weight when it walked.

The tyrannosaur had large, powerful rear legs but small front arms. These forearms wouldn't even have been able to reach its mouth. So the tyrannosaur probably planted its clawed rear feet on a dead animal, bit hard, and ripped the flesh away from the **carcass**.

The tyrannosaur is one of the most popular of all dinosaurs, thanks to films and books. But scientists still don't know a lot about the beast. Did it hunt by sight or by smell? Was tyrannosaur a hunter at all, or did it just eat the dead animals it found? Was it a fast runner?

With so many questions, we're still getting to know the tyrannosaur - but from a safe distance!

LEARN MORE! READ THESE ARTICLES…
DRAGONS (VOLUME 5) • FOSSILS (VOLUME 1)
REPTILES (VOLUME 11)

SEARCH LIGHT

Find and correct the error in the following sentence: *Tyrannosaurus rex* means 'tyrant wizard king'.

DID YOU KNOW?

Tyrannosaur fossils show features that support the theory that dinosaurs may be the distant ancestors of birds. For instance, its bones were very lightweight for their size, just as birds' are. And its walking posture resembles that of modern birds.

Sue, the famous *T. rex* in Chicago's Field Museum, was sick when she was alive. Researchers say that she suffered from gout, a painful disease that causes swelling in bones and joints.
Courtesy, Field Museum

Answer: *Tyrannosaurus rex* means 'tyrant lizard king'.

alpine relating to mountainous or hilly areas above the line where trees grow

anticlockwise in the direction opposite to the way a clock's hands move, as viewed from the front

arc a curved line

asteroid small, often rocklike heavenly body orbiting the Sun

bacterium (plural: bacteria) tiny one-celled organism too small to see with the unaided eye

canopy overhead covering

carcass dead body or leftover parts of an animal

cathedral large church where a bishop is in charge

channel lengthwise waterway that connects with other bodies of water

circulate to flow

climate average weather in a particular area

clockwise in the direction that a clock's hands move, as viewed from the front

cloudburst sudden heavy rainfall

continent one of the largest of Earth's landmasses

crude oil oil taken from the ground and not yet cleaned or separated into different products; also called petroleum

cruise a pleasure trip on a large boat or ship

debris rubbish or fragments

delta large triangular area made of material deposited at the mouth of a river, where it empties into the sea

devastate to wreck or destroy

ecosystem community of all the living things in a region, their physical environment, and all their interrelationships

element in science, one of the simplest substances that make up all matter

erode to wear down

evaporate to change into a vapour or gaseous form, usually by means of heating

evolve (noun: evolution) to change, especially over time

fossil an imprint or other trace in rock of an animal, plant, or other living thing

frigid frozen or extremely cold

gemstone natural material that can be cut and polished for use in jewellery

glacier a large river-like body of ice moving slowly down a slope or spreading over a land surface

gravity force that attracts objects to each other, keeps people and objects anchored to the ground, and keeps planets circling the Sun

habitat the physical environment in which a living thing dwells

hail small balls or lumps of ice that fall from the sky, as rain does

handiwork creative product

harness to control, much as an animal may be hitched up and controlled by its harness

hemisphere half of the planet Earth or any other globe-shaped object

horizon distant point where the land and the sky appear to meet

impression mark or figure made by pressing one object onto the surface of another; also, the effect or feeling an object or person creates

industrial having to do with businesses that construct or produce something

marine having to do with the ocean

meteorite a mass of material from space that reaches the Earth's surface

mineral substance that is not animal or plant and is an important nutrient for living things

molten melted

organism living thing

overwhelm to defeat, beat down, or swallow up

particle tiny bit or piece

peninsula a finger of land with water on three sides

pesticide poison that kills insects dangerous to growing plants

political having to do with creating and controlling a government

pollute (noun: pollution) to poison or make dirty, often with man-made waste

recycle to pass used or useless material through various changes in order to create new useful products from it

remains (noun) parts that are left after time passes or some event occurs

resort (noun) holiday centre

rotate (noun: rotation) to spin or turn

sanctuary safe place

sleet frozen or partly frozen rain

smog dirty air, a word made by combining 'smoke' and 'fog' to describe how the air looks

sonar method of locating objects (usually underwater) by sending out sound waves to be reflected back from the objects

species group of living things that have certain characteristics in common and share a name

timber wood that is cut down for use in building something

tropical having to do with the Earth's warmest and most humid (moist) climates

tyrant powerful and cruel ruler; also, someone who acts like a tyrant

vapour a substance in the state of a gas (rather than a solid or liquid)

vulnerable exposed or in danger

waste materials that are unused or left over after some work or action is finished

waterlogged filled or soaked with water and therefore heavy or hard to manage